Pronunciation Puzzles

PronPack 2
Pronunciation Puzzles

- A four-book set for teachers of English
- Fun-packed pronunciation activities
- Easy-to-follow presentation notes
- Extra resources on PronPack.com
- Print-friendly worksheets

Mark Hancock

Hancock McDonald
ENGLISH LANGUAGE TEACHING

PronPack 2
Pronunciation Puzzles

By Mark Hancock

Published by **Hancock McDonald ELT**
Chester. CH1 2AW UK
www.hancockmcdonald.com

First Published 2017

ISBN: 978-0-9957575-2-3

Contents

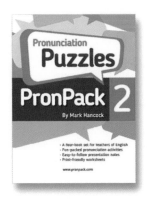

PronPack 2 Pronunciation Puzzles

PronPack 2 Activities and Worksheets

End Matter

Introduction

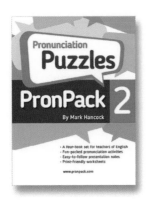

The Book

What is PronPack?

PronPack is a set of four resource books to help teachers focus on English pronunciation in class. The books contain printable worksheets along with teacher's notes explaining how to use them. Each of the four books takes a slightly different approach to pronunciation teaching. You can select the approach you prefer, or use the various books to complement one another.

What are Pronunciation Puzzles?

Pronunciation Puzzles are challenging game-like activities which are fun to do in pairs or small groups but are equally effective for individual students. They include such puzzle types as mazes, sudoku, word searches and crosswords.

What are the benefits of doing these puzzles?

The puzzles can benefit learners principally by raising awareness of patterns in the pronunciation of English such as how certain letter combinations are pronounced, where the stress falls in word families, or how words are joined together in connected speech. Although the activies are mainly concerned with awareness-raising they also provide productive rehearsal and practice for students, for example reading the words and phrases aloud while they work and when checking the answers as a class.

What aspects of pronunciation are covered?

The puzzles at the beginning of the book focus on individual sounds. The later ones focus on features such as the grammatical endings *–ed* and *–s*, suffixes and word stress, tonic stress and connected speech. In addition, since all of the words and phrases in the puzzles appear in printed form, they serve to raise awareness of sound-spelling correspondences, and reinforce the insight that English spelling does not reflect pronunciation as closely as students often expect.

What are the other books in the PronPack collection?

The three other books in the series are:

PronPack 1: Pronunciation Workouts – extended choral drill activities.

PronPack 3: Pronunciation Pairworks – communication activities.

PronPack 4: Pronunciation Poems – poems, raps and chants.

The Approach

Why teach pronunciation?

The most important reason to teach pronunciation is to help your students understand and be understood. As listeners, they need to learn how other speakers blend sounds into words and words into connected speech. As speakers, they need to modify their own accent of English to make it as widely intelligible as possible. Neither of these objectives requires them to precisely copy the accent of a native speaker. The aim is successful communication, not 'correctness'.

What is the pronunciation model?

In the context of your classroom, the best pronunciation model is almost certainly you, the teacher. PronPack aims to be as flexible as possible – you should be able to work with it whether your own accent is from London or Sydney, Turkey or Argentina. Although the phonemic symbols used are based on a British model, they are not intended to be prescriptive. For instance, /e/ does not specify the precise quality of the vowel, but merely that it is different from /æ/ or /ɪ/.

Do I have to know the phonemic alphabet?

You don't necessarily have to know or use the phonemic alphabet for most of the puzzles. Individual phoneme symbols appear in many of the games, but they are clearly exemplified and perfectly doable without prior knowledge of the symbols. The only exceptions are **2.11** and **2.12** – these are word searches and crosswords containing phonemic symbols.

Do these activities work only for one accent?

The puzzles do not restrict you to teaching in or to a General British accent – they should work for a variety of accents, including American. The phonemic spellings in **2.11** and **2.12** include symbols which are not used for American English.

However, the audio files, if you should choose to use them, are recorded in a General British accent. Note that there is both a British and an American version of the **PronPack Sound Chart**.

Note that the symbols which appear between slanted brackets in this book, such as /ʌ/ or /ʃ/, are strictly speaking, phonemes rather than sounds. A phoneme such as /ʌ/ corresponds to slightly different sounds across different accents.

Flexi notes throughout the books highlight ways that you can adapt the material to work with different accents.

The Activities

What materials are in the book?

The book contains printable worksheets for the students and teacher's notes for you. The teacher's notes highlight the teaching focus, minimum student level, and indicate printing requirements and audio files available for each activity. The notes give a short background to the pronunciation point plus a step-by-step procedure for using the activity in class.

How long do the activities take?

Each activity will typically take around 15-20 minutes of class time, although this can vary a lot depending on how thoroughly you exploit the material. If you would like to spend longer, you can combine the *puzzle* activity with a *workout*, *pairwork* or *poem* focusing on the same pronunciation point from **PronPack 1**, **3** or **4**. Recommended combinations are given in the *Lesson Plans* section, page 10 and in the **Goes well with ...** notes at the end of each activity.

Do I have to print out the worksheets?

The worksheets in *Pronunciation Puzzles* are best printed out, because this enables students to draw and write on the puzzles easily, although you could project them and do them as a whole class activity.

What level are the activities designed for?

The minimum level is indicated in the teacher's notes for each puzzle, but remember that this is a minimum level. An activity which is suitable for a pre-intermediate learner can be just as valuable for an upper intermediate learner – pronunciation often lags behind other competences because it has been neglected.

Are the activities for a specific age group or class size?

The activities are not aimed at a specific age group and benefit young learners and adults alike. The puzzles in this book function in any size of class.

What are the audio files for?

Apart from the book itself, there are audio files for most of the lessons for checking through the answers as a class. Teachers can use these if they are not confident about their own pronunciation. However, you can model the answers yourself instead of using the audio files, and this is usually the better option. You could use the audio to guide you in this rehearsal.

The Website

What will I find on the support website?

PronPack.com provides additional information for users of **PronPack** including downloadable poster versions of the *PronPack Sound Charts* and **Free** extra pronunciation activities.

If you have purchased an ePub or the print-version of this book we would like to thank you for supporting our endeavour. On the website you will have access to teacher resources to accompany the activities including:

- Print-friendly PDF files of the activity worksheets

- Slides to use during the presentation phase of the lessons

- Downloadable MP3 audio files as required

- Updates and additional materials

Note: The interactive functionality of the fixed-layout ePub will depend on your device and/or the ePub reader available for your device.

Contact us

We'd welcome your feedback on **www.pronpack.com** and invite you to share your thoughts and reactions on the book seller's website.

Please get in touch with us through our website if you have any difficulties with the material or would like to make a suggestion for another activity.

Connect with us on:

🐦 **twitter.com/pronpackbooks (@pronpackbooks)**

f **facebook.com/pronpack**

Lesson Plans

If you plan to focus on a particular pronunciation point, here are some recommended activity combinations from across the **PronPack Collection** (Books **1**, **2**, **3** and **4**):

- **Awareness of sounds: 2.1, 2.6**

- **The complete sound system: 1.1, 1.2, 1.3**

- **Long versus short vowels: 3.1** Version 1, **3.2** Version 2, **4.1**

- **The R vowels: 1.4, 2.2** Version 4, **4.3**

- **Vowels spelt with 2 letters: 1.5, 2.12, 2.2** Version 5, **4.4**

- **Short vowels: 1.6, 2.3, 3.1** Version 2, **3.3** vowel pairs, **4.2**

- **Stop consonants: 1.7, 3.4** Version 1, **3.3** consonant pairs, **4.11**

- **Fricatives and affricates: 1.8, 2.2** Version 2, **3.4** Version 3, **4.9, 4.10**

- **Semi-vowels: 2.2** Version 3, **3.4** Version 2, **4.7**

- **/l/ versus /r/: 3.2** Version 3, **3.5** Version 3, **4.8**

- **Consonant clusters: 1.9, 4.13**

- **-ed endings: 2.2** Version 6, **4.14**

- **/s/ versus /z/ and –s endings: 2.2** Version 1, **3.5** Version 2, **4.15**

- **Word stress: 2.9, 3.6**

- **Word stress families: 1.10, 2.7, 3.8, 4.16**

- **Weak forms: 1.11, 2.4** Version 2, **4.5, 4.17**

- **Rhythm: 1.12, 4.16**

- **Tonic stress: 1.13, 2.9, 3.10, 3.11, 3.12**

- **Connected speech: 2.5, 2.10, 3.9**

Goes well with ...

... These combinations are also given at the end of each activity.

 **Map of the Book**

The PronPack Sound Chart	A teaching and reference tool for the individual sounds of English, including an explanatory infographic. This book has two versions of the Chart: **IPA** with guidewords and **American** with guidewords.		
PUZZLES	**TEACHING FOCUS**	**MINIMUM LEVEL**	**ACTIVITY**
2.1 **From Head to Tail**	Sounds as opposed to spelling	Pre-intermediate	Finding a route through a maze
2.2 **Corner to Corner**	**Versions 1–5:** Sounds and spellings of: /s/ /z/; /ʃ/ /ʒ/; /w/ /j/; /ɜː/ /ɔː/; /əʊ/ /aʊ/. **Version 6:** past tense endings /d/ and /t/ linking to a vowel	Pre-intermediate	Finding routes through a maze
2.3 **Vowel Breakout**	The pronunciation of single vowel letters	Pre-intermediate	Finding a route through a maze
2.4 **Inside Out**	**Version 1:** The final **-s** morpheme. **Version 2:** Auxiliary verb stress patterns	Pre-intermediate	Finding a route through a maze
2.5 **Left to Right**	Vowel to vowel linking	Intermediate	Finding routes through a maze
2.6 **Sound Sudoku**	Sounds as opposed to spelling	Pre-intermediate	Identifying a pattern to complete a grid
2.7 **Puzzle Parquet**	**Version 1:** How suffixes affect word stress **Version 2:** Bigger word families	Intermediate - Upper intermediate	Completing a word family pattern
2.8 **Stress Jigsaw**	Contrastive stress	Intermediate	Matching sentence stems and endings
2.9 **Stress Mazes**	Word stress in 2-syllable nouns and verbs	Pre-intermediate	Finding a route through a maze
2.10 **Wrongly Written**	Connected speech	Intermediate	Identifying mistranscriptions
2.11 **Sound Soup**	**Version 1:** Silent letters **Version 2:** Homophones	Pre-intermediate - Intermediate	Identifying phonetically spelt words in a grid
2.12 **Word Chains**	The pronunciation of double vowel letters	Pre-intermediate	Doing a crossword-style puzzle

The PronPack Sound Chart

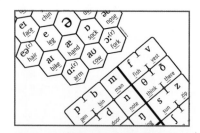

PRONPACK SOUND CHARTS

PronPack Infographic
PronPack Sound Chart 1
PronPack Sound Chart 2

What is the Sound Chart for?

Reference

The **PronPack Sound Chart** is primarily a reference tool. Teachers may print a copy as large as possible to put on the classroom wall. Whenever a pronunciation point comes up in class relating to one or more of the individual sounds, you can point it out on the chart.

Over time, the class will become more and more familiar with it. However, to get students started with the chart, you may want to devote some class time to presenting and exploring it more intensively. There are lessons focussing on the chart in **PronPack 1: Pronunciation Workouts**.

Orientation

The **PronPack Sound Chart** is intended to help you and the class find your way around the sounds of English. It enables you to see the 'big picture' – the entire system – at a glance. This is useful because if you just encounter the sounds one by one, you have no idea of where you are in the system as a whole. It could appear limitless and consequently impossible to master.

Comparison

The **PronPack Sound Chart** graphically represents relationships between the sounds, showing those that are comparable with each other and those which are very different. This helps to promote an understanding of the whole system, as well as making it more memorable. Regular users will eventually be able to remember which sound occupies which place in the chart as a whole.

How is the Sound Chart organised?

The **PronPack Sound Chart Infogaphic** on page 15 explains how the Sound Chart is organised. This is primarily for you, but you could print it out for your students at the beginning of the course too.

Note: You will find downloadable poster versions of the **PronPack Sound Charts** at **www.pronpack.com**

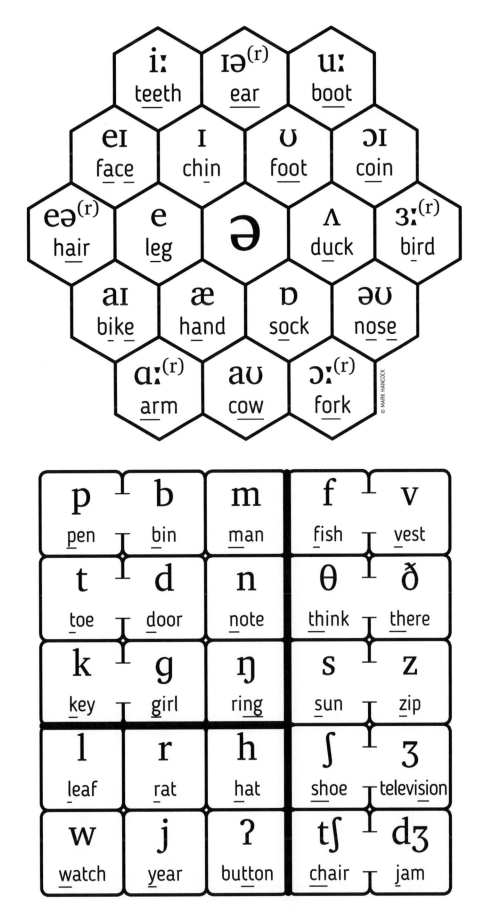

Chart 2: American Symbols with Guide Words

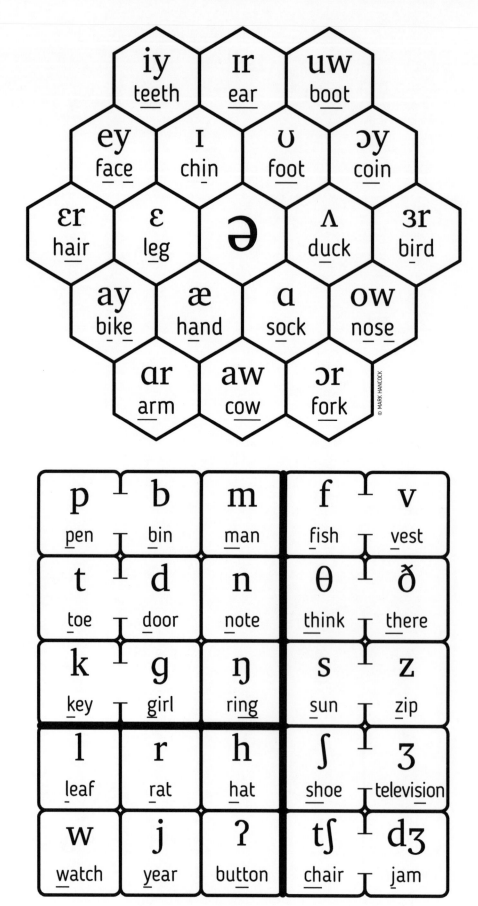

Vowels
in the hexagon...

Six Long vowels
Symbols usually have : but /eə/ also considered a long vowel in this model.

Corners

Outer Circle

Six Diphthongs
Symbols have two elements; the sound moves from one position to the other.

Sides

Six Short vowels
Symbols are all single; these vowels never end a syllable.

Inner Circle

The weak vowel
Also known as 'schwa'; only used in unstressed syllables; the most common sound in English!

Centre

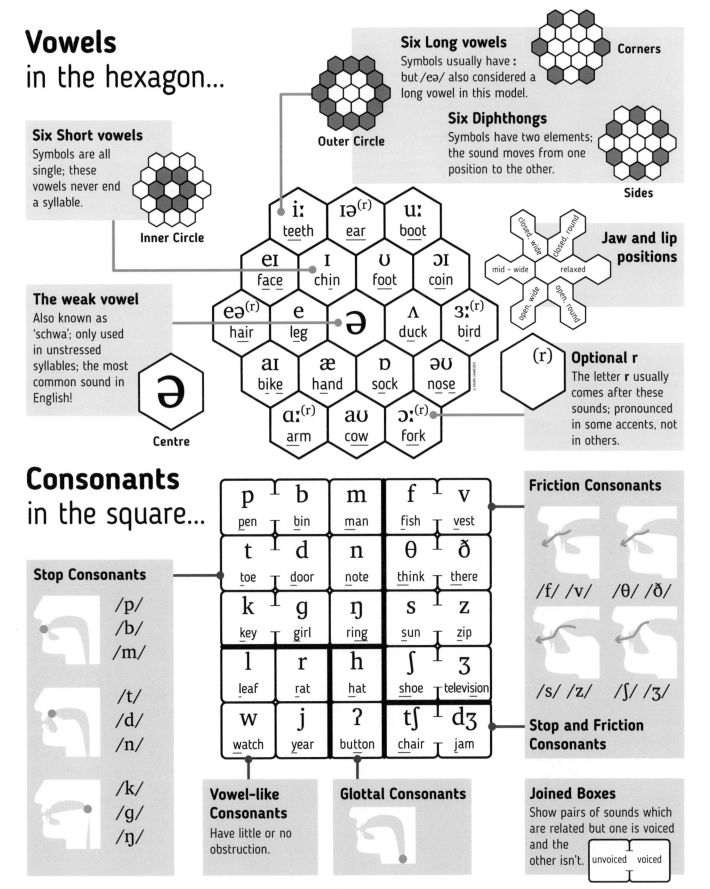

Jaw and lip positions

closed, wide | closed, round | mid - wide | relaxed | open, wide | open, round

(r) Optional r
The letter **r** usually comes after these sounds; pronounced in some accents, not in others.

Hexagon vowels:
- iː teeth
- ɪə(r) ear
- uː boot
- eɪ face
- ɪ chin
- ʊ foot
- ɔɪ coin
- eə(r) hair
- e leg
- ə
- ʌ duck
- ɜː(r) bird
- aɪ bike
- æ hand
- ɒ sock
- əʊ nose
- ɑː(r) arm
- aʊ cow
- ɔː(r) fork

© MARK HANCOCK

Consonants
in the square...

Stop Consonants

/p/
/b/
/m/

/t/
/d/
/n/

/k/
/g/
/ŋ/

Consonant square:
p pen	b bin	m man	f fish	v vest
t toe	d door	n note	θ think	ð there
k key	g girl	ŋ ring	s sun	z zip
l leaf	r rat	h hat	ʃ shoe	ʒ television
w watch	j year	ʔ button	tʃ chair	dʒ jam

Friction Consonants

/f/ /v/   /θ/ /ð/

/s/ /z/   /ʃ/ /ʒ/

Stop and Friction Consonants

Vowel-like Consonants
Have little or no obstruction.

Glottal Consonants

Joined Boxes
Show pairs of sounds which are related but one is voiced and the other isn't.
unvoiced | voiced

Pronunciation Puzzles From Head to Tail

2.1

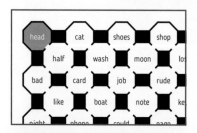

TEACHING FOCUS

To raise awareness of sounds as opposed to spelling

MINIMUM LEVEL

Pre-intermediate

ACTIVITY

Finding a route through a maze

WORKSHEETS

PronPack Worksheet 2.1
Print one copy for each student

AUDIO FILES

Background

English spelling is not phonetic. Spelling is not a reliable guide to pronunciation, although students often suppose it is. This activity forces them to notice how spelling and pronunciation diverge.

Presentation

1. Give out *Worksheet 2.1*. Write the following words on the board or direct students' attention to the words **head** and **half** in the top left-hand corner of the maze. Ask *Which sound is the same in both words?* (Answer = /h/).

   Point out that the word **head** has four letters, but only three sounds, /hed/; the word **half** also has four letters and three sounds, /hɑːf/.

2. Say the following pairs of words. Students say which sound each pair has in common.

   code – goal (= /əʊ/)
   choose – zip (= /z/)
   knife – phone (= /n/)
   join – page (= /dʒ/)
   night – buy (= /aɪ/)

   Point out how unexpected some of these are from the spelling - for example, the *–se* in **choose** is pronounced /z/.

Activity

1. Explain to students that, in this game, they begin in the room containing **head** (top left-hand corner) and have to find a way to the room containing **tail** (bottom right-hand corner). Explain that they can move in any direction but they can only move from one room to the next if the words in both have one sound in common. If you feel students need support, put them into pairs to do the activity. If students do the activity individually, they can compare in pairs before you go over the answers.

2. **Checking answers** Involve as many students as you can at this stage. Ask for a volunteer or nominate a student to say the word with a sound in **head** (half). Do not feedback immediately. Ask one or more students if they agree with the previous student's answer or if there are other answers. Repeat this procedure occasionally as you work through each of the moves. Or, you can use *Audio 2.1-1*, play and pause the audio after each word for students to check their answers as you go through the route.

Key

The sounds in common in each pair of words are shown below, underlined in **bold**:

head – **h**alf / half – c**ar**d / **c**ard – li**ke** / li**ke** – **n**ight / night – f**i**ve / **f**ive – **ph**one / phone – b**oa**t / **boa**t – job/ job – wa**sh** / wa**sh** – **sh**oes / **sh**oes – m**oo**n / m**oo**n – r**u**de / **r**ude – lo**se** / lo**se** – **z**ip / zi**p** – **k**eys / key**s** – p**ea**ce / p**ea**ce – **s**afe / safe – pa**ge** / pa**ge** – **j**oke / jo**ke** – **c**ould / could – **p**ull / pull – **c**ook / coo**k** – **p**ush / pu**sh** – **sh**eep / **sh**eep – **s**eat / sea**t** – **f**reeze / free**ze** – **l**aws / law**s** – **b**ored / bored – **f**all / fall – **s**aw / **s**aw – **v**oice / voi**ce** – **b**oys / boy**s** – **z**one / **z**one – **ch**airs / **ch**airs – **t**each / tea**ch** – **t**ail

2.1 Goes well with ...

... **PronPack 2.6** for a lesson on sound awareness.

MORE IDEAS

Students create '**word snakes**' – chains of 1-syllable words where the sound at the beginning of one word is the same as the sound at the end of the previous word, for example:

leg – go – open – nice – search – cheese – zip – plate – toy – oil – life – free – each – choose

The chain goes round the class, with each student producing a word to follw the previous student's word.

Note: Since there are no words in English beginning with /ŋ/, if anyone comes out with a word like **sing**, that's the end of the snake!

Note: In General British English, /r/ does not occur at the end of a word. For example, **car** ends with /ɑː/, so the next word should begin with this. However, if your students normally pronounce the /r/ at the end of a syllable, then the next word should begin with /r/.

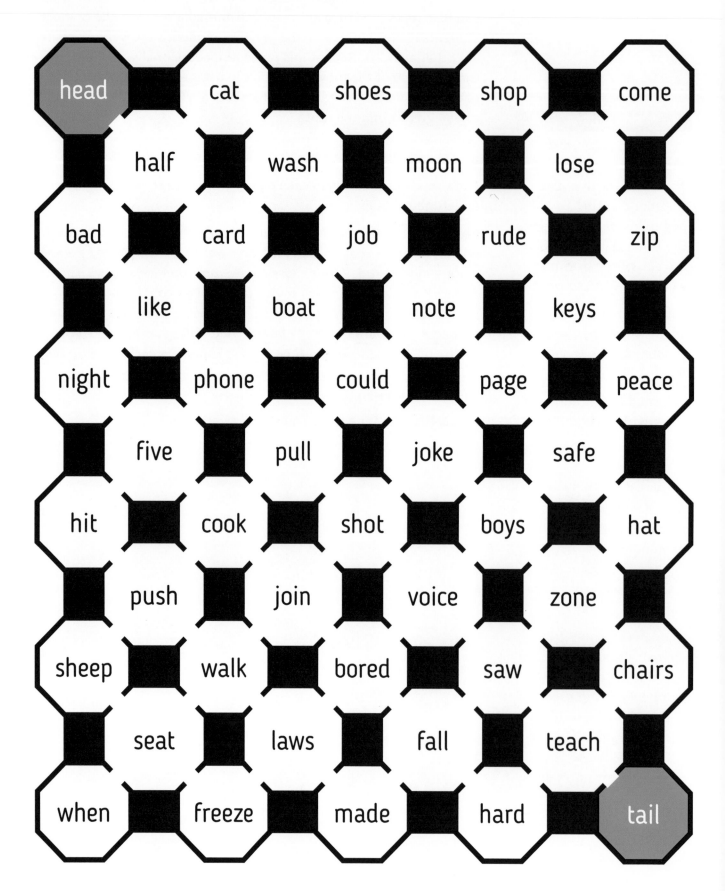

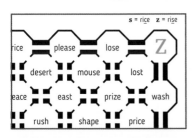

s = rice z = rise

rice · please · lose · Z
desert · mouse · lost
eace · east · prize · wash
rush · shape · price

Background

The phonemes /s/ and /z/ are familiar-looking symbols. However, they often don't correspond to the letters **s** and **z** as students might expect. For example, in **rise**, the **s** is pronounced /z/, while in **rice** the /s/ is spelt **c**. This kind of mismatch between spelling and sound is what make these puzzles challenging.

Version	1	2	3	4	5	6
Focus	/s/ and /z/	/ʃ/ and /ʒ/	/w/ and /j/	/ɜː/ and /ɔː/	/əʊ/ and /aʊ/	/d/ and /t/ (-ed endings)

Presentation

1. Write the words **rise** and **rice** on the board. Drill the pronunciation asking students to pay attention to the sound of the underlined letters. Explain that these are written /z/ and /s/ in phonetic spellings.

2. If your students have difficulty distinguishing **rise** and **rice**, explain that /z/ is voiced (you can feel the vibration of the throat) while /s/ is unvoiced. Another difference is that vowel sounds before /s/ are shorter than before /z/.

Activity

1. Give out **Version 1** of *Worksheet 2.2* and explain that the objective is to find routes between the opposite corners from **s** to **s**, and then from **z** to **z**. Check vocabulary as necessary.

2. Explain that students can go from any room to a neighbouring room with a connecting door or corridor. They can only pass through a room if the word in it contains the target sound (/s/ or /z/).

3. Go through the first few rooms together as a class (**s** – **rice** – **peace** – **east**...) and then ask students to continue, individually or in pairs.

4. Check through the *answers* together (see **Key**) or ask students to listen to *Audio 2.2-1* and check.

   Note: Follow a similar procedure for whichever version you use.

Key

The words in brackets are dead ends or alternative routes.

Version 1: (*Audio 2.2-1*) the sounds and spellings of /s/ and /z/.

s – rice – peace – east – mouse – lost – price – same – sign – face – box – ski – race – backs – fix – cats – s

z – lose – please – desert – rise – lazy – peas – news – ends – nose – phase – dogs – birds – size – bags – rays – (raise) – z

Version 2: (*Audio 2.2-2*) the sounds and spellings of /ʃ/ and /ʒ/.

ʃ – pushed – fashion – sure – cash – nation – ocean – shop – sugar – machine – patient – ship – fishing – ʃ

ʒ – casual – measure – leisure – usual – fusion – courgette – treasure – aubergine – ʒ

Version 3: (*Audio 2.2-3*) the sounds and spellings of /w/ and /j/.

w – wind – quite – queen – quick – sweet – quiz – suite – quote – swan – twice – which – quarter – white – awake – wait – w

j – cute – cure (– yellow) – queue – view – beauty – fuel – few – argue – value – Euro – youth – use – cube – j

Version 4: (*Audio 2.2-4*) the sounds and spellings of /ɜː[r]/ and /ɔː[r]/.

ɜː[r] – bird – burn – first – hurt – learn – shirt – heard – earth – nurse – word – serve – surf – worth – ɜː[r]

ɔː[r] – bored – born – force – war – door – port – short – course – warm – sport – north – sort – ɔː[r]

Version 5: (*Audio 2.2-5*) the sounds and spellings of /əʊ/ and /aʊ/.

əʊ – soap – boat – bone – coat – goal (–show) – load – rose – low – know – slow – throw – blown (– owe) – snow – grown – əʊ

aʊ – south – doubt – down – house – loud – mouth – town – now – how – sound – brown – foul (– ground) – cloud – aʊ

Version 6: (*Audio 2.2-6*) past tense endings /d‿/ and /t‿/ linking to a following vowel.

d‿ – tried on – found out – made up – turned on – saved up – called off – cried out – held up – joined up – moved in – pulled up – sold out – signed in – stayed up – tuned in – rode off – d‿

t‿ – cut off – booked up – checked in – passed out – kicked off – looked up – helped out – washed up – stopped off – jumped off – mixed up – packed up – walked out – caught on – backed up – talked up – (got up) – t‿

2.2 Goes well with ...

... **Version 1** goes well with **PronPack 1.8**, **PronPack 3.3** consonant pairs, **3.4** Version 3, **PronPack 4.9** and **4.10** for a lesson on fricatives and affricates.

... **Version 2** goes well with **PronPack 3.5** Version 2 and **PronPack 4.15** for a lesson on *s* versus *z* and *–s* endings.

... **Version 3** goes well with **PronPack 3.4** Version 2 and **PronPack 4.7** for a lesson on semi-vowels.

... **Version 4** goes well with **PronPack 1.4** and **PronPack 4.3** for a lesson on r-coloured vowels.

... **Version 5** goes well with **PronPack 1.5**, **PronPack 2.12** and **PronPack 4.4** for a lesson on vowels spelt with two letters.

... **Version 6** goes well with **PronPack 4.14** for a lesson on *–ed* endings.

2.2 Corner to Corner: Version 1

s = ri**c**e   **z** = ri**s**e

S	rice	please	lose	**Z**
	rise	desert	mouse	lost
lazy	peace	east	prize	wash
	shy	rush	shape	price
peas	news	shoe	shame	same
	sport	ends	nose	phase
school	sure	box	face	sign
	raise	ski	shine	dogs
wish	race	sugar	shoe	cash
	rays	bags	size	birds
Z	backs	fix	cats	**S**

∫ = <u>sh</u>oe   ʒ = vi<u>s</u>ion

∫

sign   sure   cash   ʒ

pushed   fashion   coast   casino

listen   past   fasten   nation   casual

savings   soap   ocean   measure

rise   sunny   shop   leisure   missing

salt   sugar   using   roses

east   sooner   mechanic   usual   news

toast   machine   fusion   music

arrange   treasure   courgette   losers   lazy

aubergine   patient   zip   magic

ʒ   orange   ship   fishing   ∫

w = <u>w</u>et   j = <u>y</u>et

W   wind   quite   queen   j

who   pay   yellow   quick

bowl   dry   dump   cure   cute

quote   suite   quiz   sweet

swan   down   boys   queue   mayor

youth   Euro   party   view

twice   which   value   whole   beauty

use   quarter   white   owe

play   sword   argue   few   fuel

cube   cow   awake   wait

j   why   day   flew   W

ɜː(r) = sh<u>ir</u>t   ɔː(r) = f<u>or</u>k

ɜː(r)	bird	born	bored	ɔː(r)
beer	burn	first	hurt	
heart	pear	force	clear	card
dark	park	star	learn	
fair	wear	war	shirt	here
where	earth	heard	stair	
beard	nurse	door	port	short
farm	steer	hear	tear	
care	word	dare	rough	course
sort	north	sport	warm	
ɔː(r)	serve	surf	worth	ɜː(r)

əʊ = n<u>o</u>s<u>e</u>   aʊ = m<u>ou</u>th

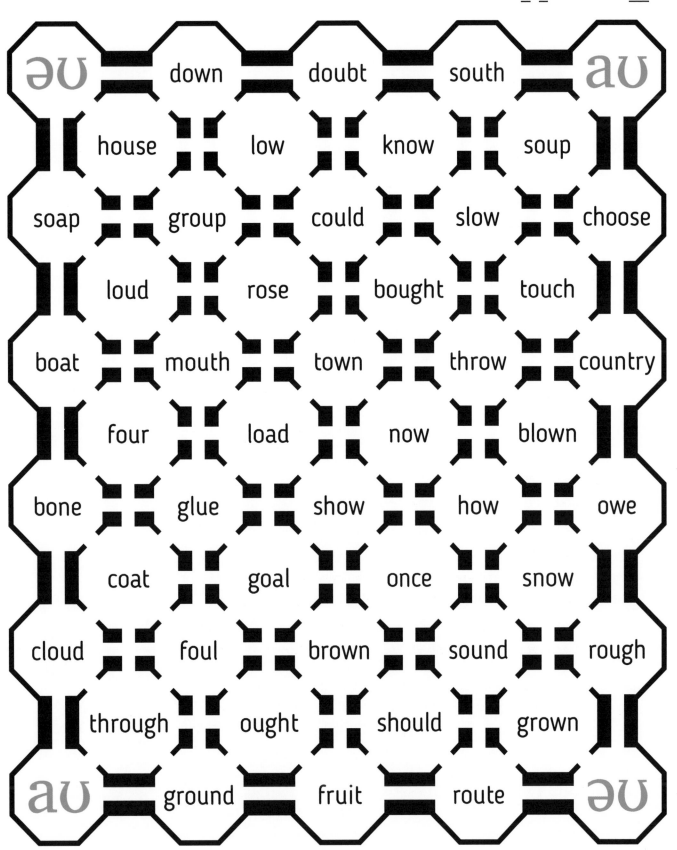

əʊ — down — doubt — south — aʊ

house · low · know · soup

soap · group · could · slow · choose

loud · rose · bought · touch

boat · mouth · town · throw · country

four · load · now · blown

bone · glue · show · how · owe

coat · goal · once · snow

cloud · foul · brown · sound · rough

through · ought · should · grown

aʊ — ground — fruit — route — əʊ

d = trie<u>d</u> on   **t** = kicke<u>d</u> off

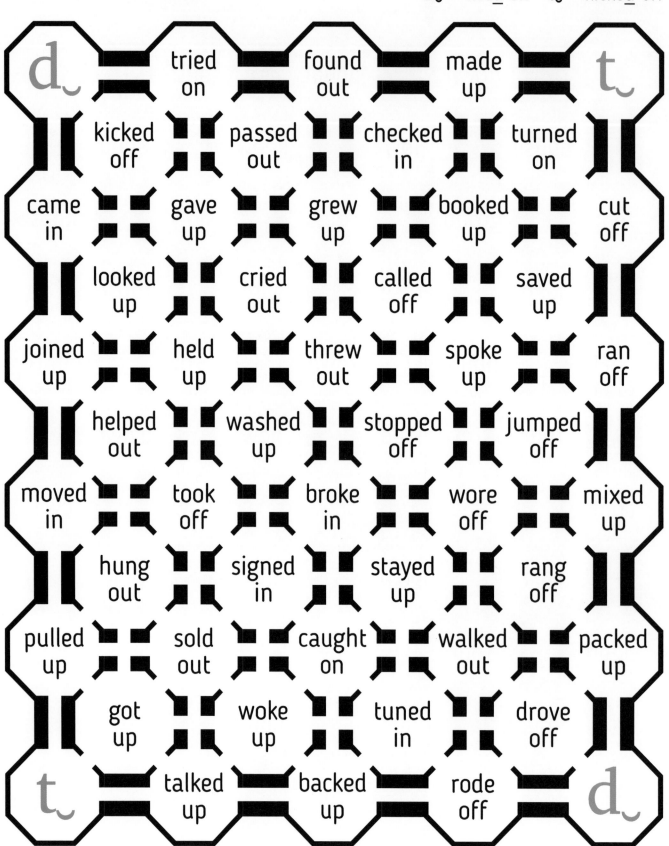

Vowel Breakout

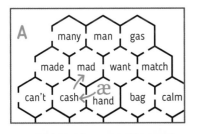

TEACHING FOCUS

To raise awareness of the pronunciation of single vowel letters

MINIMUM LEVEL

Pre-intermediate

ACTIVITY

Finding a route out of a maze

WORKSHEETS

PronPack Worksheet 2.3
Print one copy for each student or pair of students

AUDIO FILES

Background

The five vowel letters when pronounced in the alphabet are all diphthongs or long vowels. However, when you see a single vowel letter in a word (except in unstressed syllables), it has a usual short vowel pronunciation:

Vowel letters	A	E	I	O	U
Alphabet pronunciation	eɪ	iː	aɪ	əʊ	juː
Usual short vowel sound	æ	e	ɪ	ɒ	ʌ

In this game, students learn to recognise when a single vowel letter is pronounced in the typical way shown above, and the exceptions where it has a different pronunciation.

Presentation

1. Copy the vowel letters chart above on the board. For the 'usual short vowel sounds' give an example word: *hand, leg, chin, sock, duck*. Point out the spelling of the vowel sound in each of these example words – the single vowel letters *a, e, i, o,* and *u*. Explain that these are the usual pronunciations for these letters when they are on their own (i.e. not in combinations like ***ai, ea, ou*** and so on). Explain that there are exceptions to this rule though, and give these examples for each letter: *want, begin, child, cold, bull*.

   Note: The short vowel sounds do not occur at the end of words.

   Flexi: You may wish to modify the Chart above to use American symbols: /eɪ/ = /ey/, /iː/ = /iy/, /aɪ/ = /iy/, /əʊ/ = /ow/, /juː/ = /juw/, /ɒ/ = /ɑ/, /e/ = /ɛ/ and /ɒ/ = /ɑ/. If you do this, also replace the /e/ and /ɒ/ symbols on the on the worksheet.

Activity

1. Give out the *Worksheet 2.3*. Explain the object of the game is to find a way out from the middle cell to the outside of each maze.

2. Tell students they can go through any doorway if the word in the next cell has the same vowel sound as the one they start from. For example, for **Maze A**, they can go through the doorway to the ***cash***

cell because this word has the same vowel sound, but they can't go through the doorway into the **want** cell, because that word has a different vowel sound.

3. Get students to work in pairs and go through **Maze A**. The first two moves are done for them (see arrows). Encourage students to read the words aloud as they go along to check if they have the same vowel sound.

4. Go through the *answers* of **Maze A** together, and then ask the pairs to do the rest of the mazes as fast as they can.

5. Check *answers* for mazes **E, I, O, U** together or play *Audio 2.3–1* for students to check their answers.

Key

Maze A: /æ/ *hand* – *cash* – *mad* – *man* – *gas* – *match* – *bag* – *sand* – *lamb* – *fans* – *rang*

Maze E: /e/ *leg* – *west* – *left* – *fell* – *help* – *pet* – *next* – *bet* – *sent* – *egg* – *men* – *spend* – *test*

Maze I: /ɪ/ *chin* – *win* – *sing* – *miss* – *dig* – *hit* – *film* – *king*

Maze O: /ɒ/ *clock* – *song* – *boss* – *fog* – *golf* – *lost* – *rock* – *shop* – *job* – *knock* – *not* – *off*

Maze U: /ʌ/ *thumb* – *cut* – *must* – *hunt* – *sung* – *luck* – *cup* – *judge* – *lunch* – *gun* – *run*

Follow up

Ask students to look at the words which did **NOT** have the usual short vowel sound in the mazes, and ask if they can see any patterns. Here are some possibilities:

– a final **silent –e** gives the vowel its alphabet pronunciation – compare *win* and *wine*;

– vowel letters are not their usual short sound before **r, w** or **y**, and sometimes **l**;

– you never get the usual short vowel sound at the end of a word – for example: **so, ski, be**.

2.3 Goes well with...

... **PronPack 1.6**, **PronPack 3.1** Version 2, **3.3** vowel pairs and **PronPack 4.2** for a lesson on short vowels.

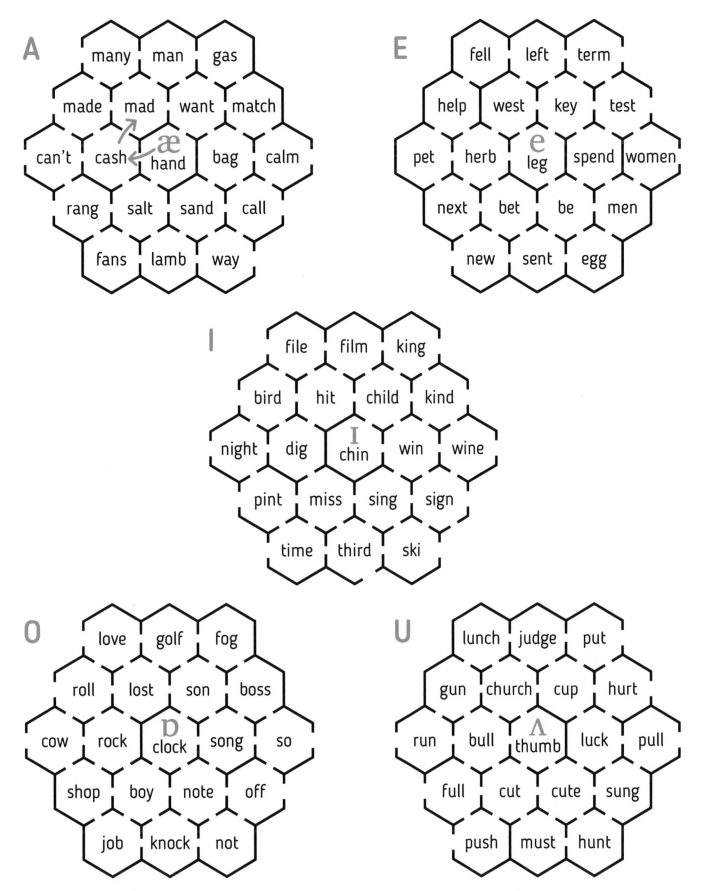

A

many — man — gas
made — mad — want — match
can't — cash — hand — bag — calm — æ
rang — salt — sand — call
fans — lamb — way

E

fell — left — term
help — west — key — test
pet — herb — e leg — spend — women
next — bet — be — men
new — sent — egg

I

file — film — king
bird — hit — child — kind
night — dig — I chin — win — wine
pint — miss — sing — sign
time — third — ski

O

love — golf — fog
roll — lost — son — boss
cow — rock — ɒ clock — song — so
shop — boy — note — off
job — knock — not

U

lunch — judge — put
gun — church — cup — hurt
run — bull — ʌ thumb — luck — pull
full — cut — cute — sung
push — must — hunt

Inside Out

2.4

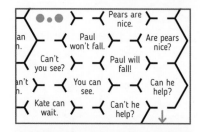

TEACHING FOCUS

Version 1: To raise awareness of the final **-s** morpheme
Version 2: Awareness of auxiliary verb stress patterns

MINIMUM LEVEL

Pre-intermediate

ACTIVITY

Finding a route through a maze

WORKSHEETS

PronPack Worksheet 2.4
Print one copy for each student or pair of students

AUDIO FILES

Background

Version 1 focuses on the **-s** morpheme. A final **-s** is used in a number of grammatical structures in English: the plural, the 3rd person of the present simple, and the possessive **'s**. In all cases, it is usually pronounced /s/ or /z/. However, the final **-s** is pronounced /ɪz/ if the root word ends with one of the following sounds: /s, z, ʃ, ʒ, tʃ, dʒ/.

Version 2 focuses on auxiliary verbs, which are normally unstressed, but stressed in the negative.

Presentation – Version 1

1. This version focuses on the final **-s** morpheme. Write the following names **Anne** and **Liz** on the board. Ask students how many syllables they contain (=**1**).

2. Now add **'s** (*Anne's*, *Liz's*). Ask students how many syllables they contain (**Anne's = 1**, **Liz's = 2**). Ask them if they can explain why there is an extra syllable in **Liz's** (because the **z** and the **s** are similar sounds, so a vowel sound is inserted to separate them).

3. Tell them that the phonetic spelling for the final syllable in **Liz's** is /ɪz/.

Activity

1. Give students **Version 1** of *Worksheet 2.4*, and explain that the objective is to find a way from the central /ɪz/ to one of the letters **A - H**. They can go through a hexagon only if the word in it ends with the syllable /ɪz/ (as in *Liz's*).

2. Go through the first couple of hexagons with the class (*oranges*, *watches*).

3. Ask them to continue finding the route.

4. Check *answers* together (see **Key**) or play *PronPack Audio 2.4-1* for students to check their answers.

Key - Version 1

The final **-s** morpheme (*PronPack Audio 2.4-1*)

ɪz – *oranges* – *watches* – *Thomas's* – *dances* – *bridges* – *Alice's* – *wishes* – *arranges* – *wages* – *switches* – *George's* – *passes* – *boxes* – *houses* – *James's* – *boss's* – *taxes* – **D**

Presentation/Activity - Version 2

1. **Version 2** focuses on the auxiliary verbs forms; *were, can, will, has* and *do*. These are normally unstressed, but stressed in the negative (*aren't, weren't* etc). Note: Auxiliary verbs are also stressed at the end of a sentence, for example "Yes, we can", but there are no examples in this activity.

2. In this version of the puzzle, students can move through a hexagon only if the sentence in it has the pattern **OoO**, as in *Jim can cook*. The circles represent syllables – big for stressed and small for unstressed.

3. Draw the following table on the board. Point out that like auxiliary verbs, pronouns are normally unstressed.

OoO	ooO	OOO
Jim can cook. Can't you see?	You can see. Can you see?	Jim can't cook.

4. Give students **Version 2** of *Worksheet 2.4* and explain that the objective is to find a way from the central **OoO** to one of the letters **A - H**. Ask them to find the route and check answers together or play *Audio 2.4.-2* for students to check their answers.

Key - Version 2

Auxiliary verb stress patterns (*Audio 2.4-2*)

OoO – *Can't you see?* – *Kate can wait.* – *Don't you know?* – *Things were fine.* – *Can't he help?* – *Paul will fall.* – *Pears are nice.* – *Weren't we quick!* – *Won't she go?* – *Mel can spell.* – *Aren't you late?* – *Chris will cook.* – *Jim can swim.* – *Joan will phone.* – *James has gone.* – *Trish can fish.* – *Joe will go.* – *Cats are cute.* – **B**

2.4 Goes well with ...

... **Version 2** goes well with **PronPack 1.11**, **PronPack 4.5** and **4.17** for a lesson on weak forms.

2.4 Inside Out: Version 1

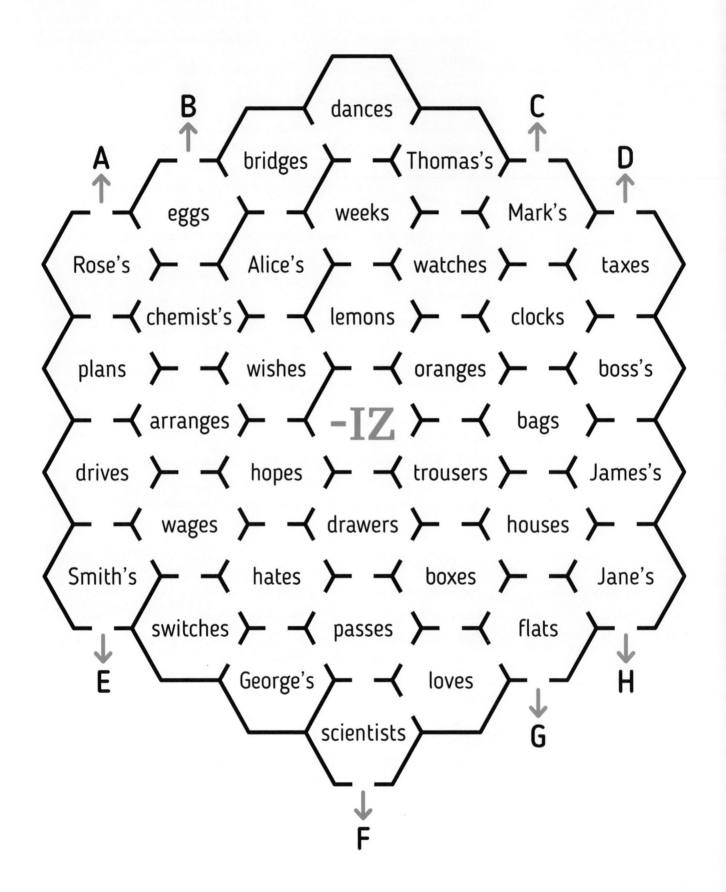

dances

B

A

C

D

bridges   Thomas's

eggs   weeks   Mark's

Rose's   Alice's   watches   taxes

chemist's   lemons   clocks

plans   wishes   oranges   boss's

arranges   **-IZ**   bags

drives   hopes   trousers   James's

wages   drawers   houses

Smith's   hates   boxes   Jane's

switches   passes   flats

E   George's   loves   H

scientists   G

F

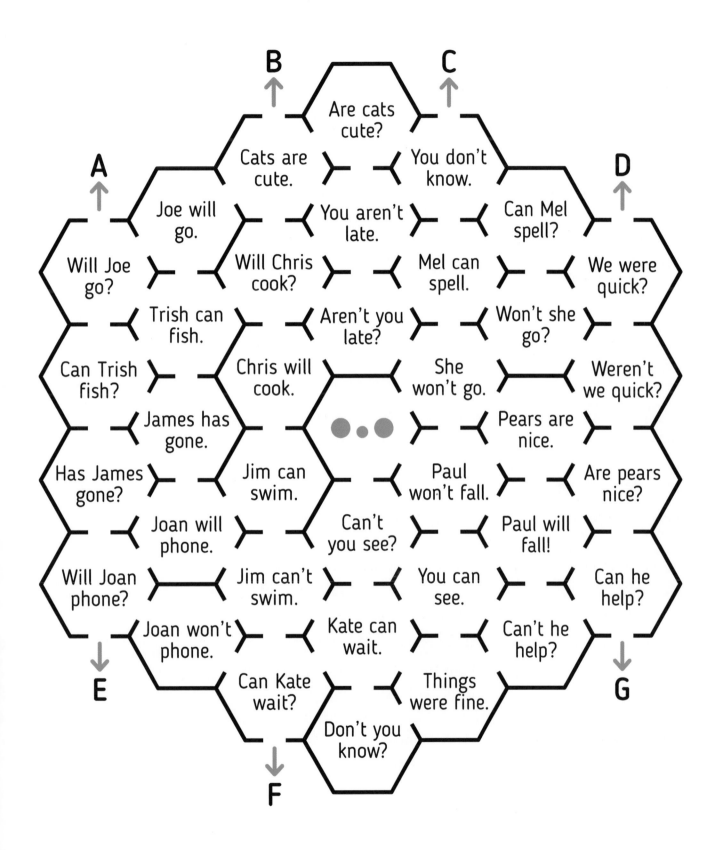

Left to Right

2.5

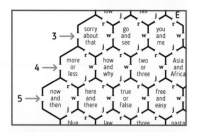

TEACHING FOCUS

To raise awareness of vowel to vowel linking

MINIMUM LEVEL

Intermediate

ACTIVITY

Finding routes through a maze

WORKSHEETS

PronPack Worksheet 2.5
Print one copy for each student or pair of students

AUDIO FILES

Background

In connected speech, there is a problem when one word finishes with a vowel sound and the next begins with a vowel sound: how do we stop the two vowel sounds blending into one? The answer is by inserting a consonant sound between the two. The linking consonant sounds are:

/r/ after /ə, ɪə, ɔː, ɜː, ɑː, eə/
/j/ after /iː, ɔɪ, aɪ, eɪ/
/w/ after /uː, əʊ, aʊ/

Students probably will not need to know the above rule - they will usually be able to work out which linking sound is needed by saying the phrase to themselves and paying attention to which sound comes naturally. They are asked to produce it in this activity, but it is not essential for them to incorporate it into their own long term pronunciation – this lesson is particularly important for raising awareness of linking in the context of listening skills.

Presentation

1. Write the following phrases on the board:
   wa<u>r</u> and peace
   da<u>y</u> and night
   ne<u>w</u> and old

   Say the words *war*, *day* and *new*. Point out that the underlined letter in each may not be pronounced (the *r* in *war* is pronounced in some accents, but not others, and the letters *y* in *day* and *w* in *new* are part of the spelling of the vowel sound). Now say the phrases and point out how the underlined letters **<u>are</u>** pronounced when the next word begins with a vowel sound.

2. Now write the following phrases on the board:
   pasta and sauce
   tea and coffee
   tomato and onion

   Say these phrases and point out that they also have the same linking consonants *r*, *y* and *w* before the word **and**, even though they are not represented at all in the spelling. Students may find this surprising.

3. Point out that the phonetic letter for the *y* sound in *yellow* is /j/.

Activity

1. Give out the *Worksheet 2.5* and explain that the objective is to get from left (the numbers) to right (the letters).

2. Tell students that they can move from hexagon to hexagon from left to right according to the linking sound in the phrase. If it is /r/, they go up, if it is /w/ they go straight on, and if it is /j/, they go down.

3. Go through the first route as an example:

   1 – *me and you* (contains /j/ link) – *buy and sell* (contains /j/ link) – *you and me* (contains /w/ link) – **F**

4. Ask students to do the remaining routes **2-9** in pairs. Point out that some of the exit letters are used more than once.

5. Check the answers and make sure students can pronounce the phrases using the linking sounds. You can play and pause *Audio 2.5-1* after each word for them to check answers as you go through the routes.

Note: Linking /j/ and /w/ are not as strong as the full phonemes. For example, The /j/ in *three or four* is not as strong as in *three your four*.

Key

2 – *high and low – go and see – you and me* – **F**

3 – *sorry about that – how and why – two or three – Asia and Africa* – **G**

4 – *more or less – sorry about that – how and why – two or three – Asia and Africa* – **G**

5 – *now and then – here and there – how and why – two or three – Asia and Africa* – **G**

6 – *blue and red – law and order – true or false – free and easy – pasta or rice – idea of fun* – **I**

7 – *now or never – four or five – three or four – happy or sad* – **O**

8 – *tea or coffee – tuna or cheese – India and China – happy or sad* – **O**

9 – *tuna or cheese – India and China – happy or sad* – **O**

2.5 Goes well with ...

... **PronPack 2.10** and **PronPack 3.9** for a lesson on connected speech.

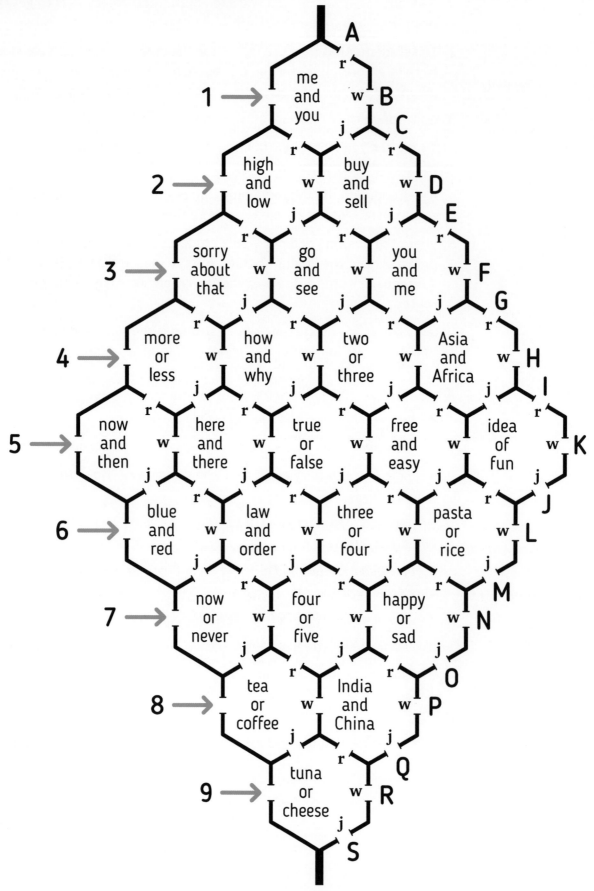

Sound Sudoku

2.6

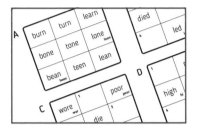

Background

The same sound in English is often spelt in a number of different ways. For example, *learn* /lɜː^(r)n/ and *burn* /bɜː^(r)n/ both have the same vowel sound /ɜː/, despite the different spelling. This game forces students to confront this fact, and analyse words by sounds rather than letters.

Presentation

Write the words *learn* and *burn* on the board. Ask them to think about the pronunciation of these two words and say what they have in common and what is different (the first consonant sound is different, the rest is the same. This is clear if you see the phonetic spellings: /lɜː^(r)n/ and /bɜː^(r)n/). Give out *Worksheet 2.6*.

Activity

1. Students look at **Game A**, which is already completed, and work out the rules: **a.** the words in each column have the same initial consonant (and final consonant if there is one); **b.** the words in each row have the same initial vowel sound (and final consonant if there is one). Explain that in some boxes, there are two words. These are homophones – they are pronounced the same as each other.

2. Do **Game B** together as a class. Elicit answers e.g. *'What is the consonant sound in the first column? (/d/). What is the ending of the word in the first row? (/ɪd/) So what is number 1?* (**did**).

3. Students work in pairs do the remaining four games. Check the answers together or play *Audio 2.6-1*. The first pair to have finished with the correct answers wins.

Key - see DIAGRAM 2.6A

Game B: **1** – did; **2** – hid; **3** – lied; **4** – dead; **5** – head

Game C: **1** – door; **2** – why; **3** – pie; **4** – day; **5** – pay

Game D: **1** – hair; **2** – share; **3** – shy; **4** – he; **5** – pea

Game E: **1** – sit; **2** – bit; **3** – hat; **4** – heat; **5** – seat

Game F: **1** – bought; **2** – bite; **3** – night; **4** – coat; **5** – note**

DIAGRAM 2.6A

A

burn	turn	learn
bone	tone	lone loan
bean been	teen	lean

B

1 did	lid	2 hid
died	3 lied	hide
4 dead	led lead	5 head

C

wore war	1 door	poor pour
2 why	die	3 pie
way weigh	4 day	5 pay

D

1 hair	pair pear	2 share
high hi	pie	3 shy
4 he	5 pea	she

E

hit	1 sit	2 bit
3 hat	sat	bat
4 heat	5 seat	beat

F

1 bought	caught	nought
2 bite	kite	3 night
boat	4 coat	5 note

MORE IDEAS

Students create small 2 x 2 Sudoku Grids following the same principle – the words start with the same sounds in the columns and end with the same sounds in the rows.

toes	nose
toys	noise

whose	use
hears	years

bike	like
bake	lake

take	cake
took	cook

2.6 Goes well with ...

... **PronPack 2.1** for a lesson on sound awareness.

A

burn	turn	learn
bone	tone	lone *loan*
bean *been*	teen	lean

B

1	lid	2
died	3	hide
4	led *lead*	5

C

wore *war*	1	poor *pour*
2	die	3
way *weigh*	4	5

D

1	pair *pear*	2
high *hi*	pie	3
4	5	she

E

hit	1	2
3	sat	bat
4	5	beat

F

1	caught	nought
2	kite	3
boat	4	5

Puzzle Parquet

2.7

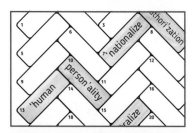

Background

We can form families of words by adding suffixes, for example, *art*, *artist*, *artistic*. Often, the stressed syllable is different across these related words because certain suffixes affect stress placement. In this example, the stress in *artistic* is different from *art* and *artist* because the suffix *-istic* causes the stress to fall on the syllable which comes before it.

Presentation

1. Write *art*, *artist* and *artistic* on the board. Say the words aloud and ask students to identify the stressed syllable in each (ˈart, ˈartist, arˈtistic). Explain that the apostrophe is the normal way to show stress in dictionaries, and it is placed at the beginning of the stressed syllable.

2. Elicit the relationship of the three words on the board (the subject/discipline; the person who does it; an adjective related to it). Explain to the students that they are going to complete a puzzle with groups of three words which have these relationships.

Activity

1. Put the students in pairs and give each pair *Worksheet 2.7* **Version 1**. Ask them to look at the word in the Parquet **Tile 1** and guess what the word in **Tile 2** is (*artist*), and the word in **Tile 3** (*artistic*). Explain that the whole pattern of tiles contains groups of words which are related in this way.

2. Ask students to complete the puzzle as quickly as possible, showing the stressed syllables with an apostrophe. The first pair to do so correctly will be the winners.

3. Go through answers together or play *Audio 2.7-1* or *Audio 2.7-2* and let students listen and check.

4. Drill the pronunciation of the word families. You can use *Audio 2.7-1* or *Audio 2.7-2* for this.

Note: Follow a similar presentation procedure for **Version 2**.

Key - Version 1:

A puzzle for Intermediate level

1 ˈart	**2** ˈartist	**3** arˈtistic
4 biˈology	**5** biˈologist	**6** bioˈlogical
7 ˈchemistry	**8** ˈchemist	**9** ˈchemical
10 ecoˈnomics	**11** eˈconomist	**12** ecoˈnomical
13 elecˈtronics	**14** elecˈtrician	**15** eˈlectrical
16 geˈography	**17** geˈographer	**18** geoˈgraphical
19 ˈhistory	**20** hiˈstorian	**21** hiˈstorical
22 matheˈmatics	**23** mathemaˈtician	**24** matheˈmatical
25 ˈmedicine	**26** ˈmedic	**27** ˈmedical
28 ˈmusic	**29** muˈsician	**30** ˈmusical
31 phiˈlosophy	**32** phiˈlosopher	**33** philoˈsophical
34 ˈphysics	**35** ˈphysicist	**36** ˈphysical
37 psyˈchology	**38** psyˈchologist	**39** psychoˈlogical
40 ˈscience	**41** ˈscientist	**42** scienˈtific

Note: economical and **physical** follow the same pattern in form as the others, but their meaning is not connected in the same way.

Key - Version 2:

A puzzle with bigger families for Upper Intermediate

1 ˈauthor	**2** auˈthority	**3** ˈauthorize	**4** authoriˈzation
5 ˈnation	**6** natioˈnality	**7** ˈnationalize	**8** nationaliˈzation
9 ˈperson	**10** persoˈnality	**11** ˈpersonalize	**12** personaliˈzation
13 ˈhuman	**14** huˈmanity	**15** ˈhumanize	**16** humaniˈzation
17 ˈcentre	**18** cenˈtrality	**19** ˈcentralize	**20** centraliˈzation
21 ˈcrime	**22** crimiˈnality	**23** ˈcriminalize	**24** criminaliˈzation
25 ˈform	**26** forˈmality	**27** ˈformalize	**28** formaliˈzation
29 ˈhospital	**30** hospiˈtality	**31** ˈhospitalize	**32** hospitaliˈzation
33 ˈlaw	**34** leˈgality	**35** ˈlegalize	**36** legaliˈzation

Note: the words in the last two columns such as **authorize** and **authorization** have an alternative possible spelling **authorise** and **authorisation** in British English.

2.7 Goes well with...

... **PronPack 1.10**, **PronPack 3.8** and **PronPack 4.16** for a lesson on word stress families.

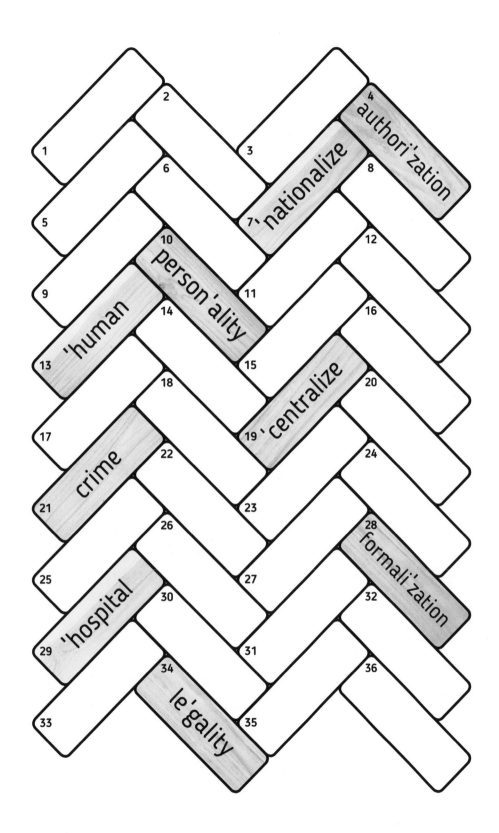

Pronunciation Puzzles

Stress Jigsaw

2.8

TEACHING FOCUS

To raise awareness of contrastive stress

MINIMUM LEVEL

Intermediate

ACTIVITY

Matching sentence stems and endings

WORKSHEETS

PronPack Worksheet 2.8
Print one copy for each student or pair of students

AUDIO FILES

Background

Spoken English can be divided into chunks, known as **tone units**. These are often full sentences, but also can be only a part of a sentence. Each tone unit has a syllable which has the main stress. This is known as *tonic stress*. In an English tone unit, the tonic stress is often placed on a word which contrasts with something said previously. In this exchange, the speaker stresses **love** in the answer to contrast with *like* in the question.

> **Question:** *Would you like to go to Brazil?*
> **Answer:** *I'd **love** to go to Brazil.*

Presentation

1. Write the short **Q/A** dialogue above on the board. Elicit from the students why the speaker stresses **love** in the answer. Drill the pronunciation of the answer.

2. Give out the *Worksheet 2.8* , point out the questions **1-12** (left) and the answers **A-L** (right). Read out the answers in random order and ask students to identify which answer you are saying, for example:

   You: *I speak English **and** Czech.*
   Students: *F !*

3. Ask for volunteers around the class to read out random answers for their classmates to identify. In order to succeed, the speaker will need to make sure that the **bolder** word is clearly stressed.

Activity

1. Explain to students that they have to join jigsaw pieces by matching questions with answers. As an example, give the first match, **1** – *B*.

2. Play the dialogues on *Audio 2.8-1* or check the *answers* together:
   1 - *B*, **2** - *K*, **3** - *C*, **4**- *J*, **5** - *D*, **6** - *L*, **7** - *A*, **8** - *I*, **9** - *G*, **10** - *E*, **11** - *H*, **12** - *F*

3. Ask students in pairs to read out the mini-dialogues, making sure they stress the **bold** word in the answers.

2.8 Goes well with ...

... **PronPack 1.13, PronPack 3.10, 3.11** and **3.12** for a lesson on tonic stress.

Question ⊐○ Answer

1 Would you like to go to Brazil?

2 What do you speak, apart from English?

A I speak **English** and Czech.

B I'd **love** to go to Brazil.

3 Istanbul's the capital of Turkey, isn't it?

4 Where did you go after university?

C No, **Ankara**'s the capital of Turkey.

D I spent **five** years in India.

5 You spent a year in India didn't you?

6 Where would you like to go to?

E I spent five **years** in India.

F I speak English **and** Czech.

7 What do you speak, apart from Czech?

8 Ankara's the capital of Iran, isn't it?

G **I'd** love to go to Brazil.

H No, Ankara's the **capital** of Turkey.

9 I'd love to visit Russia. What about you?

I No, Ankara's the capital of **Turkey**!

10 You spent five months in India, didn't you?

J I spent five years in **India**.

11 Ankara's a small place in Turkey, isn't it?

12 Do you speak English, or Czech?

K I speak English and **Czech**.

L I'd love to go to **Brazil**.

Stress Mazes

2.9

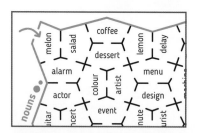

Background

Nouns with two syllables usually have the stress on the first syllable in English. This is true in about 90% of cases. For verbs, it is more common for the stress to be on the second syllable. This is true in about 60% of cases, so there are plenty of exceptions. The mazes in this activity are designed to raise awareness to these two patterns. Some of the words in the mazes may be cognates in the students' own language, but possibly with a different stress pattern.

Presentation

1. Write the following words on the board: *melon*, *prefer*. Ask students to say each one and decide if the stress pattern is **Oo** or **oO** (**Oo** for *melon* and **oO** for *prefer*).

2. Explain that these are the typical patterns for nouns and verbs – but there are plenty of exceptions!

Activity

1. Give out *Worksheet 2.9* and explain that for each maze, the objective is to find a route from the arrow going in at the top left and the arrow going out at the bottom right.

2. Explain that students may go through a '**room**' only if the word has the stress pattern which is written to the left of the mazes – **Oo** for the nouns and **oO** for the verbs.

3. Go through the first few rooms as a class (*melon – salad – coffee*) and then ask students to continue individually or in pairs.

4. Check through the *answers* (below) for each maze, together as a class or play *Audio 2.9-1* and ask students to check their own work.

   Nouns: *melon - salad - coffee - lemon - menu - artist - colour - actor - concert - college - minute - tourist - sofa*

   Verbs: *prefer - invite - collect - forget - belong - enjoy - explain - decide - compare - behave - allow - describe - escape - repeat - believe*

2.9 Goes well with ...

... PronPack **3.6** for a lesson introducing word stress.

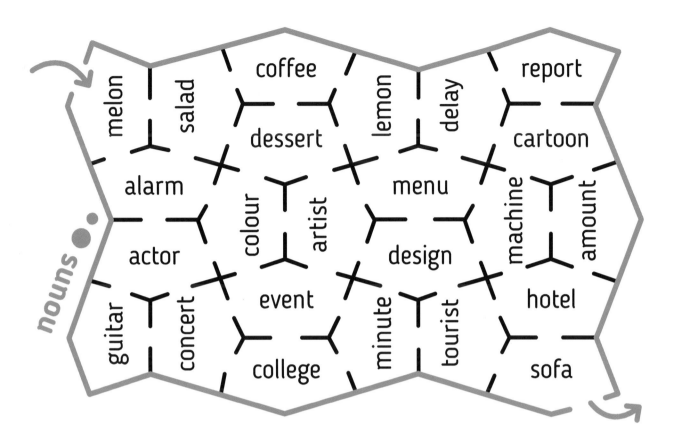

nouns ●●

melon · salad · coffee · lemon · delay · report
alarm · dessert · menu · cartoon
colour · artist · machine · amount
actor · design · hotel
guitar · event · minute · tourist
concert · college · sofa

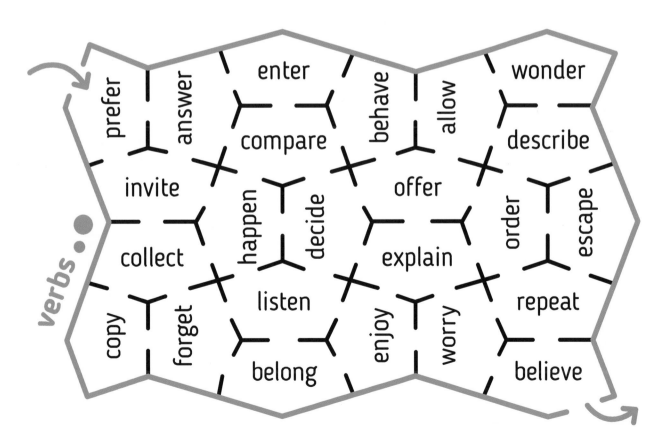

verbs ●●

prefer · answer · enter · behave · allow · wonder
invite · compare · offer · describe
happen · decide · order · escape
collect · explain
copy · listen · repeat
forget · belong · enjoy · worry · believe

Wrongly Written

2.10

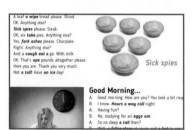

Sick spies

TEACHING FOCUS

To raise awareness of connected speech

MINIMUM LEVEL

Intermediate

ACTIVITY

Identifying mistranscriptions

WORKSHEETS

PronPack Worksheet 2.10
Print one copy for each student or pair of students

AUDIO FILES

Background

Words in context are not pronounced the same as they are in citation form (as in the dictionary). In context, they are modified: function words are reduced (weak forms), sounds change under the influence of neighbouring sounds (assimilation), sounds from one word attach to the next (linking) and sounds are deleted (elision). As a consequence, two phrases which appear completely different may in fact be homophones when said in connected speech.

For example, the two phrases below may be pronounced exactly the same (if you pronounce *address* with the stress on the 2nd syllable as in British): ***What's your address?* = *Watch or a dress?***

Presentation

1. Give out *Worksheet 2.10*, and ask students to focus on the pictures and captions first of all. Ask them to identify how the captions are wrongly written:

   Sick spies = ***Six pies***
   A way call night = ***Awake all night***
   This great eye = ***This grey tie***

2. Explain that, when spoken, these phrases sound identical. They are not mishearings. They were wrongly written down because in each case, the listener could not tell where one word finished and the next word began. In speech, words join together in one continuous flow – unlike in writing, there is no gap between them.

Activity

1. Ask students to read the dialogues or listen to *Audio 2.10–1* while reading.

2. Explain that the phrases in *italics* are written as they sound, but are wrongly written. Ask students to decide what the correct phrases should be.

3. Go through **answers** in class and ask students to suggest reasons for some of the errors. With a little thought, they are usually able to do this. It is not necessary to analyse the reasons for **all** of the errors.

4. Students work in pairs and role-play the dialogues again. Ask them to join the words together, so that what they say sounds the same as what is written.

Key

At the Deli

a wipe = **of white**
(the **of** is reduced to a; the /t/ changed to /p/ because the /b/ at the start of the next word requires closed lips)

sick spies = **six pies**
(the /s/ at the end of **six** joins the beginning of the next word)

take = **steak**
(the /s/ at the beginning of **steak** joins together with the /s/ at the end of **six**)

fork aches = **four cakes**
(the /k/ at the start of **cakes** joins to the previous word)

cough eat a = **coffee to**
(the /t/ of **to** has been heard as part of the previous word)

ape = **eight**
(the /t/ of **eight** has changed to /p/ in preparation for the next word)

a tall = **at all**
(the /t/ of at has joined the following word)

an ice = **a nice**
(the /n/ of **nice** has joined the previous word)

Good Morning

hours a way call = **I was awake all**
(**I was** is reduced and sounds like **hours**; the /k/ of **awake** has joined the next word)

eggs am = **exam**
 (one word has been heard as two)

a tall = **at all**
 (the /t/ of **at** has joined the following word)

a feller sleep = **I fell asleep**
 (the weak form of **I** sounds like **a**; the **a** at the beginning of **asleep** has joined the previous word)

a hat = **I had**

(the weak form of **I** sounds like **a**; the /d/ of **had** has changed to /t/ in preparation for the next word)

way cup = ***wake up***
(the /k/ of **wake** has joined the next word)

wait = ***eight***
(there is a linking /w/ at the start of **eight**)

fee lawful = ***feel awful***
(the /l/ of **feel** has joined the next word)

sore rise = ***sore eyes***
(the /r/ of **sore** has been pronounced and linked to the next word)

tyre doubt = ***tired out***
(the /d/ of **tired** has joined the next word)

The Birthday

part eat a night = ***party tonight***
(the /t/ of **tonight** has joined the previous word; two words have been heard as **four**)

ate a clock = ***eight o'clock***
(the /t/ of **eight** has joined the next word)

watch or a dress = ***what's your address***
(the /j/ of **your** has changed the sound of the consonants at the end of the previous word; **address** has been heard as 2 words)

Markets treat = ***Market Street***
(the /s/ of **street** has joined the previous word)

itch a birth date a day = ***it your birthday today***
(the /j/ of **your** has changed the consonant sounds at the end of the previous word; the /t/ of **today** has joined the previous word)

great eye = ***grey tie***
(the /t/ of **tie** has joined the previous word)

lie kit = ***like it***
(the /k/ of **like** has joined the next word)

suit shoe = ***suits you***
(the final /s/ of **suits** has blended with the /j/ of **you** to make a *SH* sound).

2.10 Goes well with ...

... **PronPack 2.5** and **PronPack 3.9** for a lesson on connected speech.

At the Deli...

A: Morning. What would you like?

B: A loaf **a wipe** bread please. Sliced.

A: OK. Anything else?

B: **Sick spies** please. Steak.

A: OK, six **take** pies. Anything else?

B: Yes, **fork aches** please. Chocolate.

A: Right. Anything else?

B: And a **cough eat a** go. With milk.

A: OK. That's **ape** pounds altogether please.

B: Here you are. Thank you very much.

A: Not **a tall**! Have **an ice** day!

Sick spies

A way call night!

Good Morning...

A: Good morning. How are you? You look a bit rough.

B: I know. **Hours a way call** night.

A: Having fun?

B: No, studying for an **eggs am**.

A: So no sleep **a tall** then?

B: Well, **a feller sleep** at seven and **a hat** to **way cup** at quarter to **wait**.

A: You must **fee lawful**!

B: Yes, I've got **sore rise** and I'm **tyre doubt**.

A: Well, you'd better take it easy today!

The Birthday...

A: I'm having a birthday **part eat a night**. Do you want to join us?

B: Sure. What time?

A: **Ate a clock**.

B: OK. **Watch or a dress**?

A: 15 **Markets treat**.

B: OK. Is **itch a birth date a day**?

A: Yes, it is.

B: Happy birthday! Did you get any presents?

A: Yes, I got this **great eye**. Do you **lie kit**?

B: Yes, very smart. It really **suit shoe**!

This great eye!

Sound Soup

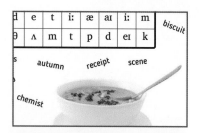

Background

English spelling is not phonetic, and many words contain letters which are not pronounced. For example, the **w** in *two* is silent. Often there are historical reasons for this, and there may be related words in which the same letter *is* pronounced – for example, the **w** in *twice*.

Students will need to have some familiarity with the phonemic alphabet in order to do this puzzle.

Presentation

Version 1: Write the word *comb* on the board along with its phonemic transcription /kəʊm/. Ask students to identify the letter of the spelling which is silent (**b**). Ask students if they can think of any more examples of words with silent letters (eg **write, half, knee**).

Version 2: Write the word *too* on the board, along with its phonemic transcription /tuː/. Ask students to give another word with the same transcription but different spelling (**two**). Tell students that words like this, with the same sound but different spellings, are called **homophones**.

Activity

1. Give out *Worksheet 2.11* to the students or pairs of students. Explain that the words around the edges are hidden in the grid, phonemically spelt.

   In **Version 1**, the example of **comb** is given, in **Version 2** the example of **too/two** is given. Note that for each word in the Homophones Soup, one of the homophones is in **A** and the other is in **B**. Check vocabulary as necessary.

2. Explain that students must find the rest of the words in the grid. It will help them to know that:
   a. All of the letters in the grid are part of a word.
   b. None of the letters in the grid are used in more than one word.
   c. All of the words are either horizontal or vertical – there are no diagonals.

3. Go through the *answers* for **Version 1** together, first horizontal then vertical words, highlighting the ***silent letters*** or use *Audio 2.11-1*.

4. For **Version 2** go through the *answers* together, first for the horizontal words and then vertical words or use *Audio 2.11-2*).

Key – Version 1

DIAGRAM 2.11A shows the completed word grid for **Version 1**. The silent letters are underlined in **bold** below.

Horizontal words

si*g*n; clim**b**; cons*c*ious; bisc*u*it; com**b**; *s*cene; de**b**t; thum**b**; ach*e*

Vertical words

c*h*emist; forei*g*n; **k**not; recei**p**t; **w**rap; g*u*ide; **k**nee; autum**n**

Note: The term 'silent letter' is not strictly accurate – the letter may show how one of the other letters in the word is pronounced. For example, the **u** in *guide* shows us that the **g** is pronounced /g/ rather than /dʒ/.

Key – Version 2

DIAGRAM 2.11B shows the completed word grid for **Version 2**. The homophones are shown in *italic*/**bold** below.

Horizontal words

lone/**loan**; *weigh*/**way**; *sale*/**sail**; *nose*/**knows**; *maid*/**made**; *meet*/**meat**; *road*/**rode**; *week*/**weak**; *toe*/**tow**; *two*/**too**; *routes*/**roots**; *rose*/**rows**; *right*/**write**; *missed*/**mist**; *war*/**wore**

Vertical words

male/**mail**; *peace*/**piece**; *weight*/**wait**; *blue*/**blew**; *would*/**wood**; *sell*/**cell**; *new*/**knew***

* the /j/ in these words is dropped in American English.

Flexi: This activity is based on British phonemes and may not work for some accents.

DIAGRAM 2.11A
Version 1: Words with silent letters

DIAGRAM 2.11A
Version 2: Homophones

Silent Letters

comb

knee

knot

sign

ache

debt

wrap

foreign

guide

biscuit

k	s	aɪ	n	k	l	aɪ	m
e	f	k	ɒ	n	ʃ	ə	s
m	ɒ	b	ɪ	s	k	ɪ	t
ɪ	r	n	r	k	əʊ	m	ɔː
s	ɪ	ɒ	ɪ	s	iː	n	t
t	n	t	s	r	g	n	ʌ
d	e	t	iː	æ	aɪ	iː	m
θ	ʌ	m	t	p	d	eɪ	k

conscious

autumn

receipt

scene

thumb

chemist

climb

Homophones

l	əʊ	n	w	eɪ	w	b	w
m	s	eɪ	l	p	eɪ	l	ʊ
eɪ	n	əʊ	z	iː	t	uː	d
l	m	eɪ	d	s	m	iː	t
r	əʊ	d	w	iː	k	t	əʊ
t	uː	r	uː	t	s	s	n
r	əʊ	z	r	aɪ	t	e	j
m	ɪ	s	t	w	ɔː(r)	l	uː

A

cell
loan
write
roots
maid
weak
maid
weigh
meet
male
weight
two
peace
nose
toe
sail
rows
missed
rode
wood
blue
knew
wore

B

too
road
new
mail
lone
blew
sell
would
right
rose
sale
made
war
wait
meat
routes
mist
tow
week
way
knows
piece

Word Chains

2.12

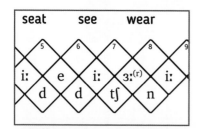

TEACHING FOCUS

To raise awareness of the pronunciation of double vowel letters

MINIMUM LEVEL

Pre-intermediate

ACTIVITY

Doing a crossword-style puzzle

WORKSHEETS

PronPack Worksheet 2.12
Print one copy for each student or pair of students

AUDIO FILES

No audio with this activity

Background

The number of vowel sounds in English far exceeds the number of vowel letters, so complex spellings are required to represent them. Many sounds are represented by double vowel letters (vowel digraphs), and of these, the combinations **ea**, **oo** and **ou** are the most problematic because they each have a number of possible pronunciations. The puzzles in this lesson raise awareness of these.

Presentation

1. Write the verb *read* on the board and ask students to pronounce it. Elicit that it has two pronunciations – /riːd/ for the present tense and /red/ for the past. Explain that the letter combination **ea** is usually pronounced /iː/ but sometimes it is pronounced /e/.

2. Write *bear*, *hear* and *heard* on the board and ask students to pronounce them. Explain that when there is a letter *r* after, *ea* is no longer /iː/ nor /e/, but one of these other three sounds /eə/, /ɪə/ or /ɜː/.

   Note: In addition to the five sounds mentioned above, **ea** may be exceptionally pronounced in other ways too: /eɪ/ in *steak* (but students probably know *break* already) and /ɑː/ in *heart*. But you don't need to bother students with these exceptions unless they ask.

Activity

1. Give out *Worksheet 2.12* and ask students to look at the top half – **EE/EA Word Chain**. Explain that they have to write one of the letters given into the numbered boxes to create the words below. Point out that the words below all contain vowel spellings **ee** or **ea**.

2. Get students started by giving them a first example. Ask them to write the symbol /h/ in **Box 5**. This creates the word **heat** going down to the left, and **head** going down to the right, in phonemic transcription. Students can now cross out the words *heat* and *head* from the list of words above.

3. Ask students to complete the rest of the puzzle in pairs. If necessary, direct them to a phonemic chart or list of phonemes in a dictionary to remind them of the symbols.

4. After going through the answers for the **EE/EA Word Chain** below, ask students to look at the **OO/OU Word Chain**.

Explain that these vowel spellings also have a number of alternative pronunciations. Ask them to solve the puzzle in a similar way to the **EE/EA Word Chain**.

Key

EE/EA Word Chain	OO/OU Word Chain
1 /d/ (dear)	**1** /w/ (wool)
2 /n/ (near, neat)	**2** /w/ (would, wound)
3 /s/ (see/sea, seat)	**3** /p/ (pool, pound)
4 /b/ (beat, bead)	**4** /s/ (sound, south)
5 /h/ (heat, head)	**5** /h/ (hound, house)
6 /r/ (read, reach)	**6** /m/ (mouth, mood)
7 /l/ (lead, learn)	**7** /g/ (goose, good)
8 /s/ (search, sea/see)	**8** /ʃ/ (should, shoot)
9 /b/ (bean, bear)	**9** /f/ (food, four)
10 /w/ (wear)	**10** /b/ (bought)

5. Ask students to look at the completed **OO/OU Word Chain** and tell you the most common pronunciation of these spellings (/aʊ/ followed by /uː/ and /ʊ/).

Note: there is one exceptional pronunciation not included in the **OO/OU Word Chain**, which is found in the words **touch** and **country**.

Flexi: This activity is based on British phonemes and may not work for some accents.

2.12 Goes well with ...

... **PronPack 1.5**, **PronPack 2.2** Version 5 and **PronPack 4.4** for a lesson on vowels spelt with two letters.

EE/EA Chain

Write these symbols in 1-10 to form the words below: b d h l n r s w

bead	bean	bear	beat	dear	head	heat
lead	learn	near	neat	reach	read	sea

search   seat   see   wear

OO/OU Chain

Write these symbols in 1-10 to form the words below: b f g h m p ∫ t w

bought	food	four	good	goose	hound
house	mood	mouth	pool	pound	shoot
should	sound	south	wool	would	wound

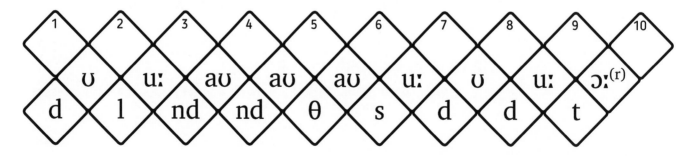

About the Author

Mark Hancock started teaching English over 30 years ago and wrote his first English language teaching book – *Pronunciation Games* – over 20 years ago. His approach in both teaching and writing ELT materials is to engage the learner and inspire their intrinsic interest in the content and in the process of the lesson. This is driven by his belief that teaching and learning a language can and should be an enjoyable experience.

He studied Geography and Philosophy at St. Andrews University, followed by teacher training courses and finally an MA in Teaching English from Aston University. Mark has taught in Sudan, Turkey, Brazil, Spain and currently lives and works in the UK. Apart from teaching and writing, he also presents at international conferences and leads on short teacher training courses.

In his free time, Mark plays the saxophone and guitar, paints in oils and walks in the mountains.

By the same author

ELT Pronunciation and Skills
- *Pronunciation Games* (CUP 1995)
- *English Pronunciation in Use Intermediate* (CUP 2003, 2012)
- *Authentic Listening Resource Pack* (Delta 2014 – co-authored with Annie McDonald)
- *Pen Pictures 1, 2 & 3* (OUP 1999 – 2000 – co-authored with Annie McDonald)
- *Oxford Advanced Learner's Dictionary 9th Ed 'Speaking Tutor' section* (OUP 2015)
- *Empower C1 'Everyday English' sections* (CUP 2016)
- *Singing Grammar* (CUP 1999)

ELT Course Book Series
- *English Result* (OUP 2007 – 2010 – co-authored with Annie McDonald)
- *Out and About* (CUP 2015 – co-authored with Annie McDonald)
- *Winners* (OUP 2010 – co-authored with Cathy Lawday)
- *New Ways to Go* (CUP 2002 – co-authored with Penny Ur and Ramon Ribé)

My first book, **Pronunciation Games**, was published back in 1995 by *CUP*. It was a photocopiable book of games with accompanying teachers' notes, designed by my sister Amanda Hancock. It seems appropriate that all these years later, my first ebooks **PronPack 1-4** should also be pronunciation activities – but printable rather than photocopiable this time – and again beautifully designed and produced by Amanda.

A huge thank you is also due to Annie McDonald for her editorial work and tireless encouragement, and to Henry Wong of Heliographic for his graphic design input.

I would also like to thank my students at *English in Chester* (www.english-in-chester.co.uk), who were the first to try out the activities in this book, and colleagues at that school who also trialled the material, especially Patsy Tyrer.

Last but not least I would like to thank my team of consultants/reviewers around the globe, including:

Freya Barua *(India)*
Marina Cantarutti *(Argentina)*
Ariel Donnell-Clark *(UK)*
Cristina Gómez Martínez *(Spain)*
Ewa Grzelak *(Poland)*
Louise Guyett de Orozco *(Ireland)*
Oksana Hera *(Ukraine)*
Stella Maris Palavecino *(Argentina)*
José Mompean *(Spain)*
Lalitha Murthy *(India)*
Catarina Pontes *(Brazil)*
Jane Neill *(UK)*
Adam Scott *(UK)*
Elena Velikaya *(Russia)*

Editor: Annie McDonald
Book design: Amanda Hancock
Graphics: Heliographic
Illustration: Mark Hancock
Images: Shutterstock.com
Audio: Mark Hancock with Annie McDonald

For more information visit **www.pronpack.com**

Notes